Welcome Little One
Baby Shower Guest Book

★★ Guests ★★

Name & relationship to parents

Advice for parents

Wishes for the baby

★★ *Guests* ★★
Name & relationship to parents

Advice for parents

Wishes for the baby

★★ Guests ★★

Name & relationship to parents

Advice for parents

Wishes for the baby

★★ Guests ★★

Name & relationship to parents

Advice for parents

Wishes for the baby

★★ Guests ★★

Name & relationship to parents

Advice for parents

Wishes for the baby

★★ *Guests* ★★

Name & relationship to parents

Advice for parents

Wishes for the baby

★★ *Guests* ★★

Name & relationship to parents

Advice for parents

Wishes for the baby

★★ Guests ★★

Name & relationship to parents

Advice for parents

Wishes for the baby

★★ *Guests* ★★

Name & relationship to parents

Advice for parents

Wishes for the baby

★★ Guests ★★

Name & relationship to parents

Advice for parents

Wishes for the baby

★★ Guests ★★

Name & relationship to parents

Advice for parents

Wishes for the baby

★★ Guests ★★

Name & relationship to parents

Advice for parents

Wishes for the baby

★★ Guests ★★

Name & relationship to parents

Advice for parents

Wishes for the baby

★★ Guests ★★

Name & relationship to parents

Advice for parents

Wishes for the baby

★★ Guests ★★

Name & relationship to parents

Advice for parents

Wishes for the baby

★★ Guests ★★

Name & relationship to parents

Advice for parents

Wishes for the baby

★★ Guests ★★

Name & relationship to parents

Advice for parents

Wishes for the baby

★★ *Guests* ★★

Name & relationship to parents

Advice for parents

Wishes for the baby

★★ Guests ★★

Name & relationship to parents

Advice for parents

Wishes for the baby

★★ Guests ★★

NAME & RELATIONSHIP TO PARENTS

ADVICE FOR PARENTS

WISHES FOR THE BABY

★★ Guests ★★

Name & relationship to parents

Advice for parents

Wishes for the baby

★★ Guests ★★

Name & relationship to parents

Advice for parents

Wishes for the baby

★★ Guests ★★

Name & relationship to parents

Advice for parents

Wishes for the baby

★★ Guests ★★

Name & relationship to parents

Advice for parents

Wishes for the baby

★★ Guests ★★

Name & relationship to parents

Advice for parents

Wishes for the baby

★★ Guests ★★

Name & relationship to parents

Advice for parents

Wishes for the baby

★★ Guests ★★

Name & relationship to parents

ADVICE FOR PARENTS

WISHES FOR THE BABY

★★ Guests ★★

Name & relationship to parents

Advice for parents

Wishes for the baby

★★ Guests ★★

Name & relationship to parents

Advice for parents

Wishes for the baby

★★ *Guests* ★★

Name & relationship to parents

Advice for parents

Wishes for the baby

★★ Guests ★★

Name & relationship to parents

Advice for parents

Wishes for the baby

★★ *Guests* ★★

NAME & RELATIONSHIP TO PARENTS

ADVICE FOR PARENTS

WISHES FOR THE BABY

★★ Guests ★★

Name & relationship to parents

Advice for parents

Wishes for the baby

★★ Guests ★★

Name & relationship to parents

Advice for parents

Wishes for the baby

★★ Guests ★★

NAME & RELATIONSHIP TO PARENTS

ADVICE FOR PARENTS

WISHES FOR THE BABY

★★ Guests ★★

Name & relationship to parents

Advice for parents

Wishes for the baby

★★ Guests ★★

Name & relationship to parents

Advice for parents

Wishes for the baby

★★ Guests ★★

Name & relationship to parents

Advice for parents

Wishes for the baby

★★ *Guests* ★★

Name & relationship to parents

Advice for parents

Wishes for the baby

★★ Guests ★★

Name & relationship to parents

Advice for parents

Wishes for the baby

★★ Guests ★★

Name & relationship to parents

Advice for parents

Wishes for the baby

★★ Guests ★★

Name & relationship to parents

Advice for parents

Wishes for the baby

★★ Guests ★★

Name & relationship to parents

Advice for parents

Wishes for the baby

★★ Guests ★★

Name & relationship to parents

Advice for parents

Wishes for the baby

★★ Guests ★★

Name & relationship to parents

Advice for parents

Wishes for the baby

★★ *Guests* ★★

Name & relationship to parents

Advice for parents

Wishes for the baby

★★ Guests ★★

Name & relationship to parents

Advice for parents

Wishes for the baby

★★ Guests ★★

Name & relationship to parents

Advice for parents

Wishes for the baby

★★ Guests ★★

Name & relationship to parents

Advice for parents

Wishes for the baby

★★ Guests ★★

Name & relationship to parents

Advice for parents

Wishes for the baby

★★ Guests ★★

Name & relationship to parents

Advice for parents

Wishes for the baby

★★ Guests ★★

NAME & RELATIONSHIP TO PARENTS

ADVICE FOR PARENTS

WISHES FOR THE BABY

★★ Guests ★★

Name & relationship to parents

Advice for parents

Wishes for the baby

★★ Guests ★★

Name & relationship to parents

Advice for parents

Wishes for the baby

★★ *Guests* ★★

Name & relationship to parents

Advice for parents

Wishes for the baby

★★ Guests ★★

Name & relationship to parents

Advice for parents

Wishes for the baby

★★ Guests ★★

Name & relationship to parents

Advice for parents

Wishes for the baby

★★ *Guests* ★★

Name & relationship to parents

Advice for parents

Wishes for the baby

★★ Guests ★★

Name & relationship to parents

Advice for parents

Wishes for the baby

★★ *Guests* ★★

Name & relationship to parents

Advice for parents

Wishes for the baby

★★ Guests ★★

Name & relationship to parents

Advice for parents

Wishes for the baby

★★ Guests ★★

Name & relationship to parents

Advice for parents

Wishes for the baby

★★ Guests ★★

Name & relationship to parents

Advice for parents

Wishes for the baby

★★ Guests ★★

Name & relationship to parents

Advice for parents

Wishes for the baby

★★ Guests ★★

Name & relationship to parents

Advice for parents

Wishes for the baby

★★ *Guests* ★★

Name & relationship to parents

Advice for parents

Wishes for the baby

★★ Guests ★★

Name & relationship to parents

Advice for parents

Wishes for the baby

★★ Guests ★★

Name & relationship to parents

Advice for parents

Wishes for the baby

★★ Guests ★★

Name & relationship to parents

Advice for parents

Wishes for the baby

★★ Guests ★★

Name & relationship to parents

Advice for parents

Wishes for the baby

★★ Guests ★★

Name & relationship to parents

Advice for parents

Wishes for the baby

★★ Guests ★★

Name & relationship to parents

Advice for parents

Wishes for the baby

★★ *Guests* ★★

Name & relationship to parents

Advice for parents

Wishes for the baby

★★ *Guests* ★★

Name & relationship to parents

Advice for parents

Wishes for the baby

★★ Guests ★★

Name & relationship to parents

Advice for parents

Wishes for the baby

★★ Guests ★★

Name & relationship to parents

Advice for parents

Wishes for the baby

★★ Guests ★★

NAME & RELATIONSHIP TO PARENTS

ADVICE FOR PARENTS

WISHES FOR THE BABY

★★ Guests ★★

Name & relationship to parents

Advice for parents

Wishes for the baby

★★ *Guests* ★★

Name & relationship to parents

Advice for parents

Wishes for the baby

★★ Guests ★★

Name & relationship to parents

Advice for parents

Wishes for the baby

★★ Guests ★★

Name & relationship to parents

Advice for parents

Wishes for the baby

★★ Guests ★★

Name & relationship to parents

Advice for parents

Wishes for the baby

★★ Guests ★★

Name & relationship to parents

Advice for parents

Wishes for the baby

★★ Guests ★★

Name & relationship to parents

Advice for parents

Wishes for the baby

★★ *Guests* ★★

Name & relationship to parents

Advice for parents

Wishes for the baby

★★ *Guests* ★★

Name & relationship to parents

Advice for parents

Wishes for the baby

★★ Guests ★★

Name & relationship to parents

Advice for parents

Wishes for the baby

★★ Guests ★★

Name & relationship to parents

Advice for parents

Wishes for the baby

★★ Guests ★★

Name & relationship to parents

Advice for parents

Wishes for the baby

★★ Guests ★★

Name & relationship to parents

Advice for parents

Wishes for the baby

★★ Guests ★★

Name & relationship to parents

Advice for parents

Wishes for the baby

★★ Guests ★★

Name & relationship to parents

Advice for parents

Wishes for the baby

★★ Guests ★★

Name & relationship to parents

Advice for parents

Wishes for the baby

★★ Guests ★★

Name & relationship to parents

Advice for parents

Wishes for the baby

★★ Guests ★★

Name & relationship to parents

Advice for parents

Wishes for the baby

★★ Guests ★★

Name & relationship to parents

Advice for parents

Wishes for the baby

★★ *Guests* ★★

Name & relationship to parents

Advice for parents

Wishes for the baby

★★ *Guests* ★★

Name & relationship to parents

Advice for parents

Wishes for the baby

★★ Guests ★★

Name & relationship to parents

Advice for parents

Wishes for the baby

★★ Guests ★★

Name & relationship to parents

Advice for parents

Wishes for the baby

★★ Guests ★★

Name & relationship to parents

Advice for parents

Wishes for the baby

★★ Guests ★★

Name & relationship to parents

Advice for parents

Wishes for the baby

★★ Guests ★★

Name & relationship to parents

Advice for parents

Wishes for the baby

★★ *Guests* ★★

Name & relationship to parents

Advice for parents

Wishes for the baby

★★ Guests ★★

Name & relationship to parents

Advice for parents

Wishes for the baby

★★ Guests ★★

Name & relationship to parents

Advice for parents

Wishes for the baby

★★ Guests ★★

Name & relationship to parents

Advice for parents

Wishes for the baby

★★ Guests ★★

Name & relationship to parents

Advice for parents

Wishes for the baby

★★ *Guests* ★★

Name & relationship to parents

Advice for parents

Wishes for the baby

★★ *Guests* ★★

Name & relationship to parents

Advice for parents

Wishes for the baby

★★ Guests ★★

Name & relationship to parents

Advice for parents

Wishes for the baby

★★ *Guests* ★★

NAME & RELATIONSHIP TO PARENTS

ADVICE FOR PARENTS

WISHES FOR THE BABY

★★ Guests ★★

Name & relationship to parents

Advice for parents

Wishes for the baby

★★ *Guests* ★★

Name & relationship to parents

Advice for parents

Wishes for the baby

★★ Guests ★★

Name & relationship to parents

Advice for parents

Wishes for the baby

★★ Guests ★★

Name & relationship to parents

Advice for parents

Wishes for the baby

★★ Guests ★★

Name & relationship to parents

Advice for parents

Wishes for the baby

★★ *Guests* ★★

Name & relationship to parents

Advice for parents

Wishes for the baby

★★ *Guests* ★★
Name & relationship to parents

Advice for parents

Wishes for the baby

★★ Guests ★★

Name & relationship to parents

Advice for parents

Wishes for the baby

★★ Guests ★★

Name & relationship to parents

Advice for parents

Wishes for the baby

★★ Guests ★★

Name & relationship to parents

Advice for parents

Wishes for the baby

★★ Guests ★★

Name & relationship to parents

Advice for parents

Wishes for the baby

★★ Guests ★★

Name & relationship to parents

Advice for parents

Wishes for the baby

★★ Guests ★★

Name & relationship to parents

Advice for parents

Wishes for the baby

★★ *Guests* ★★

Name & relationship to parents

Advice for parents

Wishes for the baby

★★ Guests ★★

Name & relationship to parents

Advice for parents

Wishes for the baby

★★ Guests ★★

Name & relationship to parents

Advice for parents

Wishes for the baby

★★ Guests ★★

Name & relationship to parents

Advice for parents

Wishes for the baby

★★ Guests ★★

Name & relationship to parents

Advice for parents

Wishes for the baby

★★ Guests ★★

Name & relationship to parents

Advice for parents

Wishes for the baby

★★ Guests ★★

Name & relationship to parents

Advice for parents

Wishes for the baby

★★ Guests ★★

Name & relationship to parents

Advice for parents

Wishes for the baby

★★ Guests ★★

Name & relationship to parents

Advice for parents

Wishes for the baby

★★ Guests ★★

Name & relationship to parents

Advice for parents

Wishes for the baby

★★ Guests ★★

Name & relationship to parents

Advice for parents

Wishes for the baby

★★ Guests ★★

Name & relationship to parents

Advice for parents

Wishes for the baby

★★ *Guests* ★★

Name & relationship to parents

Advice for parents

Wishes for the baby

★★ Guests ★★

Name & relationship to parents

Advice for parents

Wishes for the baby

★★ Guests ★★

Name & relationship to parents

Advice for parents

Wishes for the baby

★★ Guests ★★

Name & relationship to parents

Advice for parents

Wishes for the baby

★★ *Guests* ★★

Name & relationship to parents

Advice for parents

Wishes for the baby

★★ *Guests* ★★

NAME & RELATIONSHIP TO PARENTS

ADVICE FOR PARENTS

WISHES FOR THE BABY

★★ Guests ★★

Name & relationship to parents

Advice for parents

Wishes for the baby

★★ Guests ★★

Name & relationship to parents

Advice for parents

Wishes for the baby

★★ Guests ★★

Name & relationship to parents

Advice for parents

Wishes for the baby

★★ Guests ★★

Name & relationship to parents

Advice for parents

Wishes for the baby

★★ Guests ★★

Name & relationship to parents

Advice for parents

Wishes for the baby

★★ *Guests* ★★

Name & relationship to parents

Advice for parents

Wishes for the baby

www.ingramcontent.com/pod-product-compliance
Lightning Source LLC
Chambersburg PA
CBHW050713090526
44587CB00019B/3366